Margaritas, Mojitos & More

Margaritas,
Mojitos & More

BY JESSICA STRAND

PHOTOGRAPHS BY FRANKIE FRANKENY

CHRONICLE BOOKS

SAN FRANCISCO

First Chronicle Books LLC edition, published in 2008.

Text copyright © 2007 by Jessica Strand.
Photographs copyright © 2007 by Frankie Frankeny.
All rights reserved. No part of this book may be repro-
duced in any form without written permission from the
publisher.

The Library of Congress has cataloged the previous
edition as follows:
Strand, Jessica.
Margaritas, mojitos, and more / by Jessica Strand ;
photographs by Frankie Frankeny.
    p. cm.
Includes index.
ISBN 978-0-8118-5879-3 (alk. paper)
1. Margaritas. 2. Mojitos. 3. Cocktails. I. Title.
TX951.S894 2008
641.8'74—dc22
    2007042649

ISBN: 978-0-8118-6209-7

Manufactured in China

Designed by Carole Goodman / Blue Anchor Design
Food styling by Robyn Valerik and Alison Richman

The photographer wishes to thank Pamela Geismar,
Desirae Bebemiss, Chloé Harris, Christopher Sullivan,
and Windy Ferges.

The publisher wishes to acknowledge Williams-Sonoma for
providing many of the lovely pitchers, shakers, and other drink
utensils and accoutrements pictured throughout this book.

10 9 8 7 6 5 4 3

Chronicle Books LLC
680 Second Street
San Francisco, California 94107
www.chroniclebooks.com

Chambord is a registered trademark of Chatham
International, Inc., Cointreau is a registered trademark
of Cointreau Corporation, Coke is a registered trademark of
The Coca-Cola Company, Midori is a registered trademark
of Suntory Ltd., Orange Julius is a registered trademark of
Orange Julius of America, Pitu is a registered trademark
of Engarrafamento Pitu Ltda., Popsicle is a registered
trademark of Good Humor-Breyers, Toucano is a registered trademark of Wine is Fine, Inc., Wyman's is a
registered trademark of Jasper Wyman & Son.

Page 2: Citrus Crush Margarita

Dedication

To Stephen—
my mixing partner, my husband, my best friend

~~~~~~

Acknowledgments

Though the author gets credit on the cover of a book for all of her efforts, an author is nothing without a great editor—thank you Leslie Jonath. I'm forever indebted to Laurel Leigh, who manages this and other projects of mine with such finesse, grace, and competency that she makes my job a breeze. There are so many talented, terrific people involved in putting this book together without whom I'd simply be lost: Jan Hughes, Carole Goodman, Ann Rolke, Mike Ashby, Jane Chinn, thanks to each of you for your thoughtful and conscientious work! Of course, what would this book be without the keen eye of Frankie Frankeny, whose photographs make each drink look mouthwatering and beautiful—thank you, thank you. I'd like to thank my husband, Stephen Tseckares, who made it a priority to test each and every cocktail with me regardless of his crazy schedule. And, a big thanks to my son Lucian, who manned the blender and gave me tips on how to improve all the nonalcoholic smoothies. Thank you all!

Contents

I've never met a soul who doesn't love summer.

As I child, I counted the months until summer vacation. As an adult, though I live in sunny California, by February I dream of those long, warm, summer nights. Often those nights consist of a group of friends hanging out on my deck, while my husband and I blend a few fruity cocktails, kids run across the lawn, apple-turkey sausages sizzle on the grill, and the sound of voices fills the canyon where we live.

The casual fun of summer is where this cocktail book comes in handy. You'll find more than sixty easy recipes that will make any intimate or large gathering a celebration. Whether you're having a tiny soirée, a beach party, or a large barbecue, you'll find libations that will please your friends and family.

Two sections of the book feature those popular summer thirst quenchers—mojitos and margaritas. I've included the traditional recipes for these two drinks along with delicious fruit-filled versions utilizing all the fabulous seasonal fruits. Though the recipes offered are for individual servings, all of these drinks can be increased for a crowd and served pitcher-style. These flavorful cocktails might even inspire a Mexican or Cuban fiesta!

You'll also find a chapter on classic cocktails, which includes favorites like a tangy Daiquiri or creamy Piña Colada. In this group, there's also the timeless Sea Breeze, the tiki bar–standard Mai-Tai, and the popular Brazilian Caipirinha, which is similar to a mojito, but made with a richly flavored Brazilian rum.

If you're looking for new taste sensations, the "Modern Cocktails" chapter will give you a range of tempting surprises. These fusion drinks are created with flavored vodkas and sakes along with a variety of exotic ingredients. Try the clean, aromatic Cucumber-Lime Saketini or the delicate Asian Pear Martini. There's even a Lychee Gimlet and Lemon-Rosemary Saketini made with rosemary-infused lemon syrup.

And of course there are plenty of tantalizing elixirs and smoothies for people who don't want an alcoholic beverage, or for the kids looking to join in the summer festivities. My son can't get enough Blended Horchatas, and if it's not the Horchata he's asking for it's the Blueberry Crush. The elixirs are light and fresh. They're a wonderful substitute for any aperitif, as well as the perfect beverages to serve at a brunch or luncheon.

Don't waste a moment! Take out the blender and the cocktail shaker and start making your summer drinks. There's no better time to relax with friends than on a warm, clear, summer night.

BAR EQUIPMENT

Here's a simple list of bar tools that are particularly useful for making cocktails. You can serve summer cocktails in your favorite decorative glasses, but a typical glassware collection includes red wine glasses, white wine glasses, Collins glasses, margarita glasses, martini or cocktail glasses, and tumblers. And, don't forget to keep pitchers and cocktail napkins on hand.

Bar Spoon	This long-handled spoon is ideal for stirring drinks in a mixing glass, serving glass, or pitcher.
Bar Strainer	This coil-rimmed strainer is necessary for straining ice out of a mixing glass or shaker.
Bar Towel	Not just a practical accessory for wiping up spills, decorative bar towels can help you bring the holiday theme into any party.
Blender	This item is indispensable when it comes to creating summer cocktails. Nothing else works as well to combine and break down the ingredients into a smooth consistency as a good heavy duty blender.
Citrus Reamer/ Squeezer	When you're entertaining, you don't want friends to line up for a drink while you struggle to get the last bits of juice out of your citrus. These tools speed up the job.
Cocktail Picks	Wooden, plastic, metal, or bamboo skewers and toothpicks can add a delightful touch to all kinds of garnishes. Have a variety on hand to complement the different styles of glassware in your collection.
Cocktail Shaker/ Mixing Glass	This is an essential two-part item for shaking cocktails. The mixing glass serves as your container for stirred, not shaken cocktails. The cocktail shaker should have a built-in strainer; if not, make sure to buy a strainer.
Corkscrew	A basic item for any bar. Though it's typically not needed for mixing cocktails, be sure to have one on hand for recipes that require wine.

Cutting Board	A good place to do all your prepping and slicing of garnishes and other ingredients. Available in countless styles and materials, look for a small one with rubber feet to prevent sliding on a wet countertop, or place your cutting board on a bar towel.
Ice Bucket and Tongs	An ice bucket can be both a decorative and useful item to store your ice during a party so it won't melt. It can be nice to have an extra pair of tongs set out so two guests can fill their glasses at the same time.
Ice Pick/Mallet	It's nice to have something on hand to break up the ice, but certainly not essential if you are using ice cubes. To crush ice, put the chunks in a resealable plastic bag and place the bag on a hard surface that can withstand pounding. Hit the bag of ice a few times with a mallet.
Jigger Measure/ Shot Glass	This is an extremely handy item to have around, particularly for less experienced mixologists. Look for one that has half-ounce gradations to help you measure accurately.
Measuring Cups and Spoons	Most people already have these items in their kitchen. While the measuring cups are used only occasionally at the bar, the spoons will come in handy for all kinds of drink recipes.
Muddler	This wooden instrument helps to extract the juices from herbs and fruit. If a muddler isn't available you can use the back of a wooden spoon or a pestle to muddle drink ingredients. Muddling is a necessity in creating a mojito.
Sharp Knife	This is another item most people already have handy; it's essential for creating attractive garnishes.
Vegetable Peeler	Use this indispensable tool to create a twist of lemon, lime, or any other fruit with a hard skin. To make a twist, cut the skin off the fruit with a peeler, working around the circumference of the fruit.
Zester-Stripper	This is a very helpful tool that strips the rind from fruits for garnishes.

11

GARNISHES AND ADORNMENTS

The point of garnishes and adornments is to have fun with them!

Garnishes and adornments add that extra touch to any drink or cocktail. In the summertime, not only can you use fruit to top off your creation, you can add playful straws, umbrellas, and twizzle sticks. How fun is a creamy tropical smoothie topped with a bold-striped paper umbrella? Instead of using the conventional kosher white salt on your margarita rim, why not decorate with colored salt available in specialty stores—pink, purple, or pale green—depending on the flavor and color of your drink?

If you're in the mood to splurge on something a bit more exotic, top your summer cocktails with fresh edible flowers, which add a lovely, playful touch. (Make sure that they are unsprayed and always rinse before using.) What could be prettier than a pale crimson cocktail flecked with pink rose petals? Sometimes they help to enhance the flavor, but most of the time they're added to make the drink look even more festive and fanciful. So decorate away!

Since there is such a vast variety of beautiful fresh fruit available, using pieces of speared fruit makes any drink look festive. Sometimes just a simple wedge of lime or lemon or a fresh sprig of mint is all that you need. Or, freeze colorful berries or melon balls to use in place of ice.

From a flavor standpoint, garnishes for summer cocktails should be simple and straightforward. For a very sweet drink you might choose a sour adornment; for savory drinks, choose more savory adornments like pepper or cucumbers.

IDEAS FOR *GARNISHES*

- Edible flowers (hibiscus, some orchids, pansies, nasturtiums, violets, lavender, begonias, marigolds, rose petals)

- Fresh herb sprigs (mint, rosemary, tarragon, lemongrass, basil)

- Melon in tiny slices, triangles, balls (cantaloupe, honeydew, watermelon)

- Mango (slices)

- Pineapple (slices, triangles)

- Berries (raspberries, blackberries, strawberries, frozen or fresh blueberries)

- Cherries (whole, maraschino)

- Kiwi (slices or rounds)

- Kumquat (halved or whole)

- Peach (thinly sliced)

- Plum (sliced)

- Apricot (slices or rounds)

- Coconut (slice with or without husk)

- Cucumber (rounds)

- Candied fruits (ginger, mango, papaya, pineapple)

- Asian pear (slices or rounds)

- Citrus wedges, rounds, twists (lemon, lime, orange, and tangerine)

- Cinnamon (ground or stick)

- Star anise

- Whipped cream

- Shaved chocolate

IDEAS FOR *ADORNMENTS*

- Paper umbrellas

- Drink decorations: colorful plastic monkeys and mermaids to hang on the glass rim

- Paper flowers

- Fanciful straws

- Decorative glass and wooden swizzle sticks

- Colorful chopsticks

IDEAS FOR *RIMMED GLASSES*

- Colored sugar rims

- Colored salt rims

- Ground pepper

- Cinnamon-sugar

STOCKING THE SUMMER BAR

Since you may be entertaining a bit more over the summer, you'll want to stock your bar for the season. If you keep a variety of liquors and mixers on hand, you'll be ready for any spontaneous summer gatherings as well as the planned ones.

Because many of these drinks are fruit based, if you have extra limes, lemons, and a fresh juice around the house, you'll be able to whip up a variety of drinks for your drop-in visitors. However, if you want to really be prepared, try to have a supply of fresh summer fruits available and your list of drink possibilities will quadruple. (To chill glasses, place them in the freezer for fifteen minutes. Or, fill the glasses with ice water, let stand for one minute, and then pour out the ice water.)

The lists on these pages include items you'll need for mixing. They are divided into two groups, Essentials and Extras, which should help give you a sense of what is basic to make a wide variety of cocktails and what is additional for special touches. Feel free to personalize your bar by noting the kinds of drinks you and your guests prefer, and stocking it accordingly.

SUMMER MIXERS AND INGREDIENTS

Essentials

- Club soda or seltzer
- Cointreau or other orange-flavored liqueur
- Fresh or frozen fruit, such as blackberries, blueberries, mangoes, oranges, pineapples, peaches, strawberries, watermelon
- Fresh herbs and spices, such as basil, ginger, mint, lemongrass, and rosemary

- Fruit juices, such as cranberry, grapefruit, orange, pineapple, watermelon
- Gin
- Ice
- Kosher salt
- Lemons, limes, and oranges
- Whole milk

- Rum, both white (light) and dark (amber)
- Sake (store away from light and heat)
- Superfine sugar (because it dissolves more readily)
- Tequila
- Vodka, including lemon and mandarin flavors

- Cachaça
- Candied (crystallized) ginger
- Chambord or other black raspberry liqueur
- Cherry liqueur
- Coconut milk (unsweetened)
- Cream of coconut
- Crème de cassis
- Cucumbers
- Edible flowers, such as orchids, violets, pansies (look for these in the produce section of specialty stores)

- Flavored syrups, such as orange, tangerine, orgeat (almond), vanilla (look for these in coffee or dessert aisles)
- Fresh fruit, such as cantaloupe, cherries, honeydew, kiwis, kumquats, Asian pears, bananas
- Green tea
- Heavy cream
- Honey
- Jamaican rum and Limoncello or other lemon-flavored liqueur

- Maraschino cherries
- Midori or other melon-flavored liqueur
- Nectars and juices, such as blueberry, guava, hibiscus, lychee, mango, passionfruit, pear, pomegranate, tangerine, white grape
- Orange curaçao
- Peach schnapps

LIQUORS

There are many manufacturers of liquor, and you will typically find that the more you spend, the smoother and better the taste. That's not to say that a less expensive alcohol will ruin a drink. But if there is a place to spend your money on summer cocktails, this is where you want to spend it. As a rule of thumb, the fewer ingredients in the cocktail, the more the quality of the liquor matters.

You'll notice that I have chosen to specify several brand names, like Cointreau rather than Triple Sec, and Chambord rather than raspberry liqueur. I've done this because I've found that the drinks taste much smoother when using these particular brands over others.

For those liquors that you use a lot, you might want to consider purchasing larger bottles since you often get a better deal that way on the tastier brands. And don't worry about the alcohol spoiling; because of the high alcohol content of bottled spirits, they have an infinite shelf life.

SYRUPS

While you can buy many flavored syrups for drinks, some are better made from scratch. Keep these refrigerated in syrup dispensers for ease of use.

Simple Syrup

In a medium saucepan, combine 4 cups sugar and 16 ounces water. Bring the mixture to a boil over medium heat. Simmer the mixture for 3 to 5 minutes, then remove from the heat. Let the syrup cool and refrigerate in a covered container. The simple syrup lasts indefinitely. Makes 5 cups.

Basil Juice

In a small saucepan, combine 2 cups chopped basil leaves, ½ cup sugar, and 12 ounces water. Bring the mixture to a boil over medium heat. Simmer the mixture for 25 minutes, or until syrupy. Let the syrup cool. Place the mixture in a blender, and blend fully. Pour the liquid through a mesh sieve into a medium bowl. Cover and refrigerate for up to 5 days. Makes ¾ cup.

Ginger Syrup

In a small saucepan, combine 3 tablespoons grated ginger, a 2-inch chunk of peeled ginger, ¾ cup sugar, and 12 ounces water. Bring the mixture to a boil over medium heat. Simmer the mixture for 15 to 20 minutes, or until syrupy. Strain, then let cool. Cover and refrigerate for up to 1 week. Makes 1 cup.

Lemongrass Syrup

In a small saucepan, combine 3 to 4 smashed and chopped lemongrass stalks, ¾ cup sugar, and 12 ounces water. Bring the mixture to a boil over medium heat. Simmer the mixture for 30 to 40 minutes, or until syrupy. Let the syrup cool with the lemongrass, then strain. Cover and refrigerate for up to 5 days. Makes 1 cup.

Lemon-Rosemary Syrup

In a small saucepan, combine ¾ cup sugar and 6 ounces water. Set over high heat and cook, stirring occasionally, until the sugar is completely dissolved and the syrup is simmering, about 5 minutes. Remove from the heat. Add 6 ounces freshly squeezed lemon juice and ¼ cup minced rosemary to the syrup. Stir well. Strain, let cool to room temperature, then cover and refrigerate for at least 2 hours and up to 1 week. Makes 4 cups.

CLASSIC COCKTAILS

WHAT MAKES A COCKTAIL CLASSIC?
I DECIDE BASED UPON A DRINK'S
LONGEVITY, POPULARITY, AND FAMIL-
IARITY. AND IF THAT'S THE CASE, THE
COCKTAILS IN THIS CHAPTER ARE
CERTAINLY SUMMER CLASSICS WITH
THEIR WINNING FLAVORS AND THEIR
TIMELESSNESS.

RARELY ARE THESE DRINKS ALTERED.
PERHAPS A LITTLE MORE LIQUOR IS
ADDED, A TOUCH MORE LIME, AND YES,
A VARIETY OF FRUITS CAN BE SUBSTI-
TUTED, BUT THE TRADITIONAL BASE
RECIPE REMAINS THE SAME—WHY
MESS AROUND WITH A GOOD THING,
PARTICULARLY IF IT'S A CLASSIC?

Tequila Sunrise

Here is my version of a Tequila Sunrise. I use crème de cassis rather than grenadine to make the drink a bit smoother and a tad less sweet. Watch the palest yellow turn to orange and then to crimson right inside your glass.

MAKES 1 DRINK

1 cup crushed ice

2½ ounces freshly squeezed orange juice

1½ ounces tequila

1 tablespoon freshly squeezed lime juice

1 tablespoon crème de cassis

1 or 2 maraschino cherries or an orange wedge for garnish

Fill a highball glass with crushed ice. Add the orange juice, tequila, lime juice, and crème de cassis. Garnish with cherries or an orange wedge.

Cuba Libre

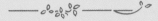

Legend has it that a soldier fighting the Spanish-American war in Cuba invented this simple drink. The soldier asked a bartender to make him a rum and Coke with a twist of lime, other soldiers ordered the same drink, and the Cuba Libre ("Free Cuba!") was born.

MAKES 1 DRINK

Ice cubes

1 ½ ounces white rum

¼ lime

Cola

Fill a highball glass with ice. Add the rum, squeeze in the lime and drop it into the drink, and add cola to taste. Stir well.

Mai-Tai

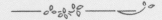

This exotic-sounding drink was actually created in 1944 by Victor "Trader Vic" Bergeron at the first Trader Vic's restaurant in Oakland, California. Jamaican rum, processed a bit differently than other rums, has a very deep, full-bodied flavor. Its dark color comes from added molasses (rather than from the cask).

MAKES 1 DRINK

Ice cubes

1 ¼ ounces freshly squeezed lime juice

1 ounce Jamaican rum

1 ounce white rum

1 tablespoon orange curaçao

1 tablespoon Simple Syrup (page 16)

1 ½ teaspoons orgeat (almond-flavored) syrup

1 sprig mint for garnish

1 edible orchid for garnish

Put a handful of ice in a cocktail shaker. Pour the lime juice, both rums, curaçao, simple syrup, and orgeat syrup over the ice. Shake vigorously and strain into a chilled highball glass. Garnish with a mint sprig and edible orchid.

Frozen Pineapple-Passionfruit Daiquiri

— ❦ —

WHILE YOU'RE SIPPING THIS FRUITY DRINK, YOU'LL FEEL MILES AND MILES FROM HOME. YOU CAN'T HELP BUT IMAGINE THAT YOU'RE ON A LUSH ISLAND, SURROUNDED BY RIPE, TROPICAL FRUIT AND BRILLIANT, NEON-COLORED FLOWERS, WITH THE COOL SEA BREEZE BLOWING THROUGH YOUR HAIR . . . YOU'RE ONE DAIQUIRI AWAY FROM PARADISE.

MAKES 1 DRINK

2 ounces passionfruit nectar

½ cup peeled, cubed fresh pineapple

1¾ ounces white rum

½ ounce freshly squeezed lime juice

1 cup crushed ice

1 wedge pineapple, peeled, and/or white edible orchid for garnish

Combine the passionfruit nectar, pineapple, rum, and lime juice in a blender and add the ice. Blend until smooth. Pour the mixture into a chilled cocktail, wine, or champagne glass. Garnish with a pineapple wedge and edible orchid.

Piña Colada

You know it's a classic if everyone wants to take credit for its creation. The name in English ("strained pineapple") sounds much less appealing than the frothy, desirable Piña Colada. Two bars in Puerto Rico have yet to settle the dispute on whether it was created by bartender Don Ramón Portas Mingot in 1963, or a decade before by bartender Ramón Marrero.

MAKES 1 DRINK

1 ½ ounces pineapple juice

1 ½ ounces dark rum

1 tablespoon cream of coconut

1 ½ teaspoons heavy cream

1 cup crushed ice

1 wedge pineapple for garnish

1 maraschino cherry for garnish

1 orange slice for garnish

Pour the pineapple juice, rum, cream of coconut, and cream into a blender. Add the ice. Blend the ingredients until smooth. Pour into a chilled festive cocktail glass. Spear the fruit together with a toothpick. Garnish with the fruit spear.

Rum Sour

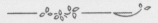

AFTER A HOT DAY IN THE SUN, SHAKE YOURSELF ONE OF
THESE DIVINE MOUTH-PUCKERING COCKTAILS. GRAB YOUR-
SELF A COMFY CHAIR, A HANDFUL OF ROASTED PEANUTS,
AND RELAX!

MAKES 1 DRINK

Ice cubes

1¾ ounces white rum

¾ ounce freshly squeezed
lemon juice

¾ ounce Simple Syrup
(page 16)

1 maraschino cherry for
garnish

Put a handful of ice in a cocktail
shaker. Pour the rum, lemon juice, and
simple syrup over the ice. Shake vigorously until frothy. Strain the drink
into a chilled sour glass and garnish
with a cherry.

Sea Breeze

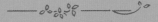

JUST THE NAME PUTS YOU IN THE MOOD FOR SUMMER.
THIS COCKTAIL HAS JUST THE RIGHT BALANCE OF
TANGY AND SWEET. USE YOUR FAVORITE VODKA OR, IF
YOU'RE LOOKING FOR A DELICIOUS TWIST, TRY ORANGE-
FLAVORED VODKA.

MAKES 1 DRINK

Ice cubes

3 ounces freshly squeezed grapefruit juice

2 ounces sweetened cranberry juice

1 ½ ounces vodka

1 lime wedge for garnish

Put a handful of ice in a cocktail shaker. Pour the grapefruit juice, cranberry juice, and vodka over the ice. Shake until blended. Strain the drink into a chilled tumbler or highball glass and garnish with a lime wedge.

10 oz.
9 oz.
8 oz.
7 oz.
6 oz.
5 oz.
4 oz.
3 oz.
2 oz.

Classic Frozen Daiquiri

SOME FEEL THAT THE FROZEN DAIQUIRI IS A BASTARDIZA-
TION, BUT NO ONE CAN ARGUE THERE'S NOTHING QUITE
AS THIRST QUENCHING ON A HOT, STICKY, SUMMER
DAY AS AN ICY, SMOOTH DAIQUIRI.

MAKES 1 DRINK

1 cup crushed ice

1¾ ounces white rum

1 tablespoon Cointreau or
other orange-flavored liqueur

½ ounce freshly squeezed
lime juice

2 teaspoons superfine sugar

1 lime slice for garnish

Combine the ice, rum, Cointreau, lime juice, and sugar in a blender. Blend at low speed, then turn to high until smooth. Pour the mixture into a chilled cocktail, wine, or champagne glass. Garnish with a lime slice.

Frozen Strawberry Daiquiri

THE ADDITION OF STRAWBERRIES GIVES THIS TANGY
DRINK A FULLER FLAVOR AND A WONDERFUL SCENT.

MAKES 1 DRINK

1 cup crushed ice

7 large fresh strawberries

1¾ ounces white rum

1 tablespoon Cointreau or
other orange-flavored liqueur

½ ounce freshly squeezed
lime juice

2 teaspoons superfine sugar

Combine the ice, 6 of the berries, the rum, Cointreau, lime juice, and sugar in a blender. Blend at low speed, then turn to high until smooth. Pour the mixture into a chilled cocktail, wine, or champagne glass. Slice the remaining strawberry halfway up from the bottom. Rest the berry on the side of the glass.

Frozen Banana Daiquiri

BY ADDING THE BANANA TO THIS CITRUS-BASED DRINK, SUDDENLY THE CONSISTENCY IS CREAMY. THE INTENSE BANANA FLAVOR REMINDS ME OF THOSE SWEATY HOT DAYS AS A KID WHERE ALL I CRAVED WAS A BANANA POPSICLE.

MAKES 1 DRINK

1 cup crushed ice

1 medium banana, cut into sixths

1¾ ounces white rum

1 tablespoon Cointreau or other orange-flavored liqueur

½ ounce freshly squeezed lime juice

2 teaspoons superfine sugar

One 2-inch piece banana, peeled, or 1 wedge pineapple, peeled, for garnish

Combine the ice, banana, rum, Cointreau, lime juice, and sugar in a blender. Blend until smooth. Pour the mixture into a chilled cocktail, wine, or champagne glass. Garnish with a banana piece or pineapple wedge.

Caipirinha

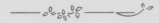

CAIPIRINHA, WHICH IN PORTUGUESE MEANS "COUNTRY BUMPKIN," IS BRAZIL'S NATIONAL DRINK. CAIPIRINHAS ARE MADE WITH CACHAÇA LIQUOR, WHICH IS OFTEN REFERRED TO AS "BRAZILIAN RUM." UNLIKE RUM, WHICH IS MADE FROM MOLASSES, CACHAÇA IS MADE FROM UNREFINED SUGARCANE. THERE ARE TWO BRANDS AVAILABLE IN THE STATES: ONE IS PITU AND THE OTHER IS TOUCANO.

MAKES 1 DRINK

2 small limes, cut into wedges

2 teaspoons superfine sugar

Ice cubes

2 ounces cachaça

Place the lime wedges in a rocks glass. Sprinkle the sugar over them. Using the back of a spoon or a muddler, crush the limes and sugar together until the sugar dissolves. Add a handful of ice to the glass. Top with the cachaça and stir.

Planter's Punch

THIS DRINK DATES BACK TO SUGARCANE PLANTATION
DAYS. IT'S BEEN AROUND FOREVER FOR A REASON . . .
IT'S SIMPLY DELICIOUS.

MAKES 1 DRINK

1 cup crushed ice

3 ounces freshly squeezed
orange juice

1½ ounces white rum

1½ ounces dark rum

1 ounce freshly squeezed
lime juice

½ ounce Simple Syrup
(page 16)

1 orange slice for garnish

1 pineapple wedge, peeled,
for garnish

1 maraschino cherry for
garnish

Combine the ice, orange juice, both
rums, lime juice, and simple syrup in
a cocktail shaker. Shake well and pour
into a tall, chilled Collins glass. Spear
the fruit together with a toothpick.
Garnish with the fruit spear.

MARGARITAS

THERE ARE FOUR TALES ABOUT THE INVENTION OF THIS DRINK, AND NO ONE IS CERTAIN WHICH IS RIGHT. HERE ARE A COUPLE OF POSSIBLE TRUTHS ABOUT THE DRINK: IT WAS INVENTED BETWEEN 1938 AND 1948, AND IT WAS CONCOCTED BY AN INGENIOUS LATINO BARTENDER EITHER IN BAJA, CALIFORNIA, OR TEXAS. WHETHER OVER ICE OR FROZEN, IT HAS REMAINED ONE OF AMERICA'S FAVORITE COCKTAILS. WHILE IT IS TRADITIONAL TO SALT THE RIM OF A MARGARITA GLASS, FEEL FREE TO OMIT THIS STEP ACCORDING TO INDIVIDUAL TASTES.

Classic Margarita

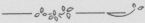

HERE'S MY ROCKS VERSION OF THE MUCH-COVETED COCKTAIL! YOU CAN SERVE MARGARITAS IN ANY FESTIVE GLASSES, WHICH MAKES FOR GREAT FUN AT THEMED PARTIES. OPTIONALLY, GARNISH WITH LIME SLICES DROPPED INTO THE DRINK FOR AN ADDED SPLASH OF FLAVOR AND COLOR.

MAKES 1 DRINK

2 lime wedges

1 tablespoon kosher salt

1 ounce freshly squeezed lime juice

2 ounces gold tequila

1 ounce Cointreau or other orange-flavored liqueur

Ice cubes

Moisten the outer rim of a chilled margarita or martini glass with 1 of the lime wedges. Spread the salt on a shallow plate and dip the glass in the salt, covering it with a light band. Set the glass aside.

Pour the lime juice, tequila, and Cointreau over a handful of ice in a shaker. Shake until very cold. Strain into the prepared glass and garnish with a lime wedge.

Passionfruit Margarita

———— ❦ ————

THIS DRINK IS AS WONDERFUL TO SMELL WITH ITS TROPICAL
PERFUME AS IT IS TO SIP WITH ITS EXOTIC, COMPLEX
TROPICAL FLAVOR THAT IS SWEET AND TART AT THE SAME
TIME.

MAKES 1 DRINK

2 lime wedges

1 tablespoon kosher salt

1 cup crushed ice

½ cup passionfruit nectar

1 ounce freshly squeezed
lime juice

2 ounces gold tequila

1 ounce Cointreau

Moisten the outer rim of a chilled
margarita or martini glass with 1 of
the lime wedges. Spread the salt on a
shallow plate and dip the glass in
the salt, covering it with a light band.
Set the glass aside.

In a blender, combine all of the ingredients except the remaining lime
wedge. Blend at high speed until
smooth. Pour into the prepared glass
and garnish with a lime wedge.

Watermelon-Ginger Margarita

THE SWEET, REFRESHING TASTE OF THE WATERMELON BLENDS BEAUTIFULLY WITH THE SUBTLE HEAT OF GINGER. I LIKE TO GARNISH THIS DRINK WITH A SPEAR OF CRYSTALLIZED GINGER AND A COUPLE TINY WEDGES OF WATERMELON.

MAKES 1 DRINK

1 lime wedge

1 tablespoon kosher salt

1 cup crushed ice

½ cup peeled, cubed watermelon, plus 1 wedge, peeled, for garnish

2 ounces gold tequila

1 ounce freshly squeezed lime juice

1 ounce Cointreau

¼ teaspoon minced fresh ginger

1 or 2 pieces candied (crystallized) ginger for garnish

Moisten the outer rim of a chilled margarita or martini glass with the lime wedge. Spread the salt on a shallow plate and dip the glass in the salt, covering it with a light band. Set the glass aside.

In a blender, combine the ice, cubed watermelon, tequila, lime juice, Cointreau, and minced ginger. Blend at high speed until smooth. Pour into the prepared glass. Garnish with a spear of crystallized ginger and watermelon.

Mango Margarita

———— ✤ ————

WHEN THE MANGOES ARE NICE AND RIPE THIS DRINK IS
PERFECT. WATCH OUT! IT TASTES LIKE A RICH, CREAMY
SMOOTHIE, BUT IT'S SPIKED WITH PLENTY OF TEQUILA.

MAKES 1 DRINK

1 lime wedge

1 tablespoon kosher salt

1 cup crushed ice

½ cup peeled, cubed mango,
plus 1 or 2 wedges for garnish

2 ounces gold tequila

1 ounce freshly squeezed
lime juice

1 ounce Cointreau

Moisten the outer rim of a chilled
margarita or martini glass with the
lime wedge. Spread the salt on a
shallow plate and dip the glass in the
salt, covering it with a light band.
Set the glass aside.

In a blender, combine the ice, cubed
mango, tequila, lime juice, and
Cointreau. Blend at high speed until
smooth. Pour into the prepared glass.
Garnish with a mango wedge or two.

Honeydew~Mint Margarita

———— ⦿⦿⦿⦿ ———— ⦿

This dreamy combination is so delicate and fresh that you'll want more than just one. Make sure you use a ripe honeydew—the ripeness of the fruit makes an enormous difference in the flavor of the drink.

MAKES 1 DRINK

1 lime wedge

1 tablespoon kosher salt

1 cup crushed ice

½ cup peeled, cubed honeydew

2 ounces gold tequila

1 ounce freshly squeezed lime juice

1 ounce Cointreau

½ teaspoon minced fresh mint, plus 1 sprig for garnish

Moisten the outer rim of a chilled margarita or martini glass with the lime wedge. Spread the salt on a shallow plate and dip the glass in the salt, covering it with a light band. Set the glass aside.

In a blender, combine the ice, honeydew, tequila, lime juice, Cointreau, and minced mint. Blend at high speed until smooth. Pour into the prepared glass. Garnish with a mint sprig.

Lemongrass Margarita

I GOT THE IDEA FOR THIS DRINK FROM A LEMONGRASS MARGARITA I HAD AT THE SABA BLUE WATER CAFE IN AUSTIN, TEXAS. I ADDED THE COINTREAU TO GIVE THE DRINK A SLIGHTLY ORANGE FLAVOR. IT'S LOVELY TO DECORATE THIS PALE, ELEGANT COCKTAIL WITH A STALK OF LEMONGRASS.

MAKES 1 DRINK

1 lime wedge

1 tablespoon kosher salt

Ice cubes

2 ounces gold tequila

1 to 1½ ounces Lemongrass Syrup (page 16)

1 ounce Cointreau

One 4- to 4½-inch stalk lemongrass for garnish

Moisten the outer rim of a chilled margarita or martini glass with the lime wedge. Spread the salt on a shallow plate and dip the glass in the salt, covering it with a light band. Set the glass aside.

Fill a cocktail shaker with a handful of ice. Pour the tequila, lemongrass syrup, and Cointreau over the ice. Shake the mixture well and strain into the prepared glass. Garnish with a stalk of lemongrass.

Peach-Strawberry Margarita

—⸰⸰⸰⸰⸰⸰— ⸰⸰

HERE'S A LITTLE TWIST ON THE EVER-POPULAR STRAW-
BERRY MARGARITA—IT'S GOT PEACHES! THE COMBINA-
TION OF PEACHES AND STRAWBERRIES MAKES THIS DRINK
TASTE AND SMELL OF SUMMER.

MAKES 1 DRINK

1 lime wedge

1 tablespoon kosher salt

1 cup crushed ice

¼ cup peeled, cubed peach,
plus 1 slice for garnish

2 teaspoons Simple Syrup
(page 16)

¼ cup hulled, quartered
strawberries, plus 2 whole
for garnish

1 ounce freshly squeezed
lime juice

1 ounce gold tequila

1 ounce peach schnapps

Moisten the outer rim of a chilled
margarita or martini glass with the
lime wedge. Spread the salt on a
shallow plate and dip the glass in the
salt, covering it with a light band.
Set the glass aside.

In a blender, combine the ice, peach
cubes, simple syrup, quartered strawberries, lime juice, tequila, and schnapps.
Blend at high speed until smooth.
Pour into the prepared glass. Spear a
strawberry, then the peach slice, then
a strawberry. Garnish with the fruit spear.

Basil-Lime Margarita

— ❦ —

I TRIED A NONALCOHOLIC VERSION OF THIS DRINK AT A
RESTAURANT IN LOS ANGELES, AND DECIDED TO TRY TO
SPIKE IT. WHAT A CLEAN, FRESH COCKTAIL IT MAKES! IT
MAY BE THE BEST IN THE BOOK!

MAKES 1 DRINK

1 lime wedge

1 tablespoon kosher salt

Crushed ice

2 ounces gold tequila

1 ounce Basil Juice (page 16)

1 ounce freshly squeezed
lime juice

1 ounce Cointreau

1 sprig basil for garnish

Moisten the outer rim of a chilled margarita or martini glass with the lime wedge. Spread the salt on a shallow plate and dip the glass in the salt, covering it with a light band. Set the glass aside.

Fill a cocktail shaker with ice. Pour the tequila, basil juice, lime juice, and Cointreau over the ice. Shake the mixture well, and strain into the prepared glass. Garnish with a basil sprig.

Plum Pucker Margarita

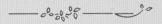

THIS IS A DRINK FOR THOSE WHO LOVE A TART, FRUITY, COOL COCKTAIL. THE ADDITION OF CHERRY LIQUEUR GIVES IT THAT EXTRA TWANG. I USE THE SILVER TEQUILA TO GET A SMOOTH, LESS INTENSE FLAVOR.

MAKES 1 DRINK

2 lime wedges

1 tablespoon kosher salt

1 cup crushed ice

½ cup peeled, pitted ripe black plums, plus 2 slices for garnish

2 ounces silver tequila

1 ½ ounces freshly squeezed lime juice

½ ounce cherry liqueur

Moisten the outer rim of a chilled margarita or martini glass with 1 of the lime wedges. Spread the salt on a shallow plate and dip the glass in the salt, covering it with a light band. Set the glass aside.

In a blender, combine the ice, ½ cup plums, tequila, lime juice, and cherry liqueur. Blend at high speed until smooth. Pour into the prepared glass. Spear a plum slice, then the remaining lime wedge, then a plum slice. Garnish with the fruit spear.

Sour Cherry Margarita

— ༺ ༻ —

You can use sour or sweet cherries when making this drink. If I'm using sweet cherries, I add a bit more lime and a little cherry liqueur to create a sour cherry flavor.

MAKES 1 DRINK

1 lime wedge

1 tablespoon kosher salt

1 cup crushed ice

½ cup pitted, ripe cherries, plus 1 whole for garnish

2 ounces silver tequila

1½ ounces freshly squeezed lime juice

½ ounce Cointreau (optional)

Moisten the outer rim of a chilled margarita or martini glass with the lime wedge. Spread the salt on a shallow plate and dip the glass in the salt, covering it with a light band. Set the glass aside.

In a blender, combine the ice, the ½ cup cherries, tequila, lime juice, and Cointreau (if using). Blend at high speed until very smooth. Pour into the prepared glass. Garnish with the whole cherry.

Blueberry Margarita

————— ❦ —————

YOUR LIPS WILL TURN A LIGHT PURPLE WHEN YOU SIP
ON THIS DREAMY SUMMER LIBATION. BLUEBERRIES ARE
RARELY USED IN MARGARITAS, BECAUSE THEY'RE A
NORTHERN FRUIT. BUT NORTH AND SOUTH BLEND BEAU-
TIFULLY IN THIS SUPERB COCKTAIL.

MAKES 1 DRINK

1 lime wedge

1 tablespoon kosher salt

1 cup crushed ice

½ cup fresh or frozen
blueberries

2 ounces gold tequila

1 ounce freshly squeezed
lime juice

1 ounce Cointreau

1 sprig mint for garnish

Moisten the outer rim of a chilled margarita or martini glass with the lime wedge. Spread the salt on a shallow plate and dip the glass in the salt, covering it with a light band. Set the glass aside.

In a blender, combine the ice, blueberries, tequila, lime juice, and Cointreau. Blend at high speed until smooth. Pour into the prepared glass. Garnish with a mint sprig.

Tropical Fruit Margarita

———◦◦◦◦———◦◦

IF YOU LOVE THE TASTE OF PIÑA COLADA, BUT YOU'RE NOT
A FAN OF RUM, HERE IS YOUR ANSWER. BECAUSE TEQUILA
IS LESS SWEET THAN RUM, YOU'LL FIND THIS DELIGHTFUL
DRINK A BIT SUBTLER THAN ITS RUM EQUIVALENT.

MAKES 1 DRINK

1 lime wedge

1 tablespoon kosher salt

1 cup crushed ice

2 ounces gold tequila

1 ounce cream of coconut

1 ounce pineapple juice

1 ounce freshly squeezed
lime juice

1 tablespoon Cointreau or
other orange-flavored liqueur

2 small pineapple wedges
for garnish

1 maraschino cherry for
garnish

Moisten the outer rim of a chilled
margarita or martini glass with the
lime wedge. Spread the salt on a
shallow plate and dip the glass in the
salt, covering it with a light band.
Set the glass aside.

In a blender, combine the ice, tequila,
cream of coconut, pineapple juice,
lime juice, and Cointreau. Blend at
high speed until smooth. Pour into
the prepared glass. Spear a pineapple
wedge, then the cherry, then a
pineapple wedge. Garnish with the
fruit spear.

Raspberry Margarita

FOR THOSE WHO LOVE COSMOPOLITANS, THIS MARGARITA
MAY BE YOUR FAVORITE. THOUGH IT SHARES ONLY TWO
OF THE SAME INGREDIENTS AND IS FROZEN RATHER THAN
SHAKEN, IT FEELS LIKE A DISTANT COUSIN WITH ITS
CRIMSON HUE AND ITS DELICATE FINISH.

MAKES 1 DRINK

1 lime wedge

1 tablespoon kosher salt

1 cup crushed ice

½ cup fresh raspberries, plus
3 to 5 whole (depending on
size) for garnish

1½ ounces gold tequila

1 ounce freshly squeezed
lime juice

1 ounce Chambord or other
raspberry liqueur

1 tablespoon cranberry juice

Moisten the outer rim of a chilled
margarita or martini glass with the
lime wedge. Spread the salt on a
shallow plate and dip the glass in the
salt, covering it with a light band.
Set the glass aside.

In a blender, combine the ice, the ½ cup
raspberries, tequila, lime juice,
Chambord, and cranberry juice. Blend
at high speed until smooth. Pour into
the prepared glass. Spear the remaining
raspberries so that they are stacked
one on top of another. Garnish with
the raspberry spear.

Citrus Crush Margarita

Part Orange Julius, part orange Popsicle! You'll love the burst of refreshing citrus flavor in this variation (pictured on page 2).

MAKES 1 DRINK

1 lime wedge

1 tablespoon kosher salt

1 cup crushed ice

1 ½ ounces gold tequila

1 ounce freshly squeezed orange juice

1 ounce freshly squeezed grapefruit juice

1 ounce freshly squeezed lime juice

1 ounce Cointreau

Orange or lime slices for garnish

Moisten the outer rim of a chilled margarita or martini glass with the lime wedge. Spread the salt on a shallow plate and dip the glass in the salt, covering it with a light band. Set the glass aside.

In a blender, combine the ice, tequila, juices, and Cointreau. Blend at high speed until smooth. Pour into the prepared glass. Garnish with the fruit slices.

MOJITOS

THERE'S A LIVELY DEBATE AMONG COCKTAIL HISTORIANS AS TO WHEN THE MOJITO WAS INVENTED AND BY WHOM. SOME BELIEVE THE DRINK ORIGINATED IN CUBA IN THE LATE NINETEENTH CENTURY. THE STORY I LIKE BEST IS THAT IT WAS A CONCOCTION DEVELOPED IN THE 1500S BY THE ENGLISH PIRATE RICHARD DRAKE, WHO, ALONG WITH OTHER TREASURE SEEKERS, INTRODUCED THE DRINK TO CUBA, THE CARIBBEAN, AND LATIN AMERICA.

Classic Mojito

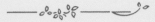

THIS CUBAN CLASSIC BLENDS TWO OF THE MOST
REFRESHING, TANTALIZING FLAVORS—LIME AND MINT.
IT'S LIGHT, EFFERVESCENT, SLIGHTLY TART, AND A
TINY BIT SWEET, MAKING IT ONE OF THE SUMMER'S
MOST SATISFYING DRINKS.

MAKES 1 DRINK

½ ounce freshly squeezed lime juice

1 teaspoon superfine sugar

5 mint leaves, plus 1 sprig for garnish

Crushed ice

2 ounces white rum

1 ounce club soda

Put the lime juice and sugar in a highball or other glass. Stir until the sugar is dissolved. Add the mint leaves and crush or muddle them against the glass with the back of a spoon or a muddler. Fill the glass with crushed ice. Add the rum and club soda, and stir gently. Garnish with a mint sprig.

Honeydew Mojito

This beautiful, pale, seafoam-green mojito is a bit sweeter and a little fuller in flavor than the original, but no less refreshing. Some refer to it as "the nectar of the gods." Use a cheese slicer or a French mandolin to cut decorative melon ribbons for added garnishment

MAKES 1 DRINK

½ cup peeled, cubed honeydew

½ ounce freshly squeezed lime juice

1 teaspoon superfine sugar

5 mint leaves (green or purple), plus 1 sprig for garnish

Crushed ice

2 ounces white rum

1 ounce club soda

Melon ribbons for garnish (optional)

Place the honeydew in a blender. Blend the fruit until it's smooth, about 2 minutes. Put the lime juice and sugar in a highball or other glass. Stir until the sugar is dissolved. Add the 5 mint leaves and crush or muddle them against the glass with the back of a spoon or a muddler. Fill the glass with crushed ice. Add the pulverized honeydew, then the rum and club soda, and stir vigorously. Garnish with mint and a few melon ribbons (if using).

Watermelon Mojito

I FIRST TASTED THIS MOJITO IN MIAMI, AND HAVE BEEN MAKING IT EVER SINCE. I USE FRESH WATERMELON JUICE INSTEAD OF BLENDING FRESH WATERMELON, BECAUSE THE JUICE IS READILY AVAILABLE AT HEALTH FOOD STORES HERE. HOWEVER, IF YOU CAN'T FIND FRESH WATERMELON JUICE JUST SUBSTITUTE ½ CUP CUBED WATERMELON AND FOLLOW THE HONEYDEW MOJITO RECIPE (PAGE 63). SERVE THIS DELICIOUS DRINK AT YOUR NEXT EVENING SOIRÉE.

MAKES 1 DRINK

½ ounce freshly squeezed lime juice

1 teaspoon superfine sugar

5 mint leaves, plus 1 sprig for garnish

Crushed ice

4 ounces fresh watermelon juice

2 ounces white rum

1 ounce club soda

2 to 3 tiny watermelon wedges, peeled, for garnish (optional)

Put the lime juice and sugar in a high-ball or other glass. Stir until the sugar is dissolved. Add the mint leaves and crush or muddle them against the glass with the back of a spoon or a muddler. Fill the glass with crushed ice. Add the watermelon juice, rum, and club soda, and stir vigorously. Spear the tiny watermelon wedges (if using), creating a stack. Garnish with the watermelon spear and mint sprig.

Mango Mojito

This mojito is the richest and thickest of the bunch. It's also the most filling; think of this as a tropical dessert drink like a Piña Colada or a Banana Daiquiri. I'm not implying that it goes at the end of the meal, I'm just saying that it's as filling as dessert. Drink up!

MAKES 1 DRINK

½ ounce freshly squeezed lime juice

1 teaspoon superfine sugar

5 mint leaves, plus 1 sprig for garnish

Crushed ice

4 ounces mango nectar

2 ounces white rum

1 ounce club soda

1 mango slice, peeled, for garnish

1 lime wedge for garnish

Put the lime juice and sugar in a highball or other glass. Stir until the sugar is dissolved. Add the mint leaves and crush or muddle them against the glass with the back of a spoon or a muddler. Fill the glass with crushed ice. Add the mango nectar, rum, and club soda, and stir vigorously. Fold the mango slice in half and spear it with a toothpick; place the lime wedge on top. Garnish with the mango and lime spear and a mint sprig.

Pineapple Mojito

— ⚜ — ⚘

THE COMBINATION OF MINT AND PINEAPPLE MAKES THIS
SUMMERY COOLER LIGHT, BUBBLY, AND A PERFECT
THIRST QUENCHER FOR A BALMY DAY. DRINK UP!

MAKES 1 DRINK

½ ounce freshly squeezed
lime juice

1 teaspoon superfine sugar

5 mint leaves, plus 1 sprig
for garnish

Crushed ice

4 ounces pineapple juice

2 ounces white rum

1 ounce club soda

1 wedge pineapple, unpeeled,
for garnish

Put the lime juice and sugar in a
highball or other glass. Stir until the
sugar is dissolved. Add the mint leaves
and crush or muddle them against
the glass with the back of a spoon or
a muddler. Fill the glass with crushed
ice. Add the pineapple juice, rum,
and club soda, and stir vigorously.
Cut the pineapple wedge at the apex
of the triangle, and place it on the side
of the glass. Finish the garnish with a
mint sprig.

Blueberry Mojito

———— ❧❧❧ ———— ❧

This pale, violet-blue mojito has a subtle, delicate flavor. Try adding whole blueberries to the drink as a garnish. They'll sink to the bottom of the glass and give your last several sips a burst of blueberry flavor. Blueberry juice is found in health food stores across the country; Wyman's is a brand that distributes everywhere.

MAKES 1 DRINK

½ ounce freshly squeezed lime juice

1 teaspoon superfine sugar

5 mint leaves, plus 1 sprig for garnish

Crushed ice

4 ounces unsweetened blueberry juice

2 ounces white rum

1 ounce club soda

4 to 6 fresh or frozen blueberries for garnish (optional)

Put the lime juice and sugar in a highball or other glass. Stir until the sugar is dissolved. Add the mint leaves and crush or muddle them against the glass with the back of a spoon or a muddler. Fill the glass with crushed ice. Add the blueberry juice, rum, and club soda, and stir vigorously. Drop the blueberries (if using) in the glass. Garnish with a mint sprig.

Cantaloupe Mojito

Lime and cantaloupe are a natural combination and enhanced with the addition of mint, the flavors create a divine cocktail. I sometimes like to spear three fresh melon balls topped with a wedge of lime for garnish.

MAKES 1 DRINK

½ cup peeled, cubed ripe cantaloupe, plus 1 small wedge for garnish

½ ounce freshly squeezed lime juice

1 teaspoon superfine sugar

5 mint leaves, plus 1 sprig for garnish

Crushed ice

2 ounces white rum

1 ounce club soda

1 lime slice for garnish

Place the ½ cup cantaloupe in a blender. Blend the fruit until it's smooth, about 2 minutes. Put the lime juice and sugar in a highball or other glass. Stir until the sugar is dissolved. Add the 5 mint leaves and crush or muddle them against the glass with the back of a spoon or a muddler. Fill the glass with crushed ice. Add the pulverized cantaloupe, then the rum and club soda, and stir vigorously. Garnish with the melon wedge, lime slice, and mint.

Strawberry Mojito

STRAWBERRIES ADD A FESTIVE DIMENSION TO THIS DRINK, GIVING IT A BRILLIANT ROSY COLOR. THE RIPER THE STRAWBERRIES, THE BETTER THE DRINK!

MAKES 1 DRINK

5 large strawberries, trimmed, plus 2 for garnish

½ ounce freshly squeezed lime juice

1 teaspoon superfine sugar

5 mint leaves, plus 1 sprig for garnish

Crushed ice

2 ounces white rum

1 ounce club soda

1 lime wedge for garnish

Place 5 of the strawberries in a blender. Blend the fruit until it's smooth, about 2 minutes. Put the lime juice and sugar in a highball or other glass. Stir until the sugar is dissolved. Add the mint leaves and crush or muddle them against the glass with the back of a spoon or a muddler. Fill the glass with crushed ice. Add the pulverized strawberries, then the rum and club soda, and stir vigorously. Spear a strawberry, then the lime wedge, then another strawberry on a toothpick. Garnish with the strawberry spear and a mint sprig.

Blackberry Mojito

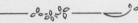

THIS DRINK IS VERY RUSTIC; YOU'LL ALMOST TASTE THE
SEEDS OF THE BLACKBERRIES AND TINY BITS OF THE SOFT
BERRY SKIN. THIS DRINK REMINDS ME OF HOMEMADE
FRUITY LEMONADES THAT I USED TO MAKE AS A KID.

MAKES 1 DRINK

½ ounce freshly squeezed lime juice

2 teaspoons superfine sugar

¼ cup blackberries

5 mint leaves, plus 1 sprig for garnish

Crushed ice

2 ounces white rum

1 ounce club soda

1 lime wedge for garnish

Put the lime juice and sugar in a highball or other glass. Stir until the sugar is dissolved. Add the blackberries and crush them against the glass with the back of a spoon or a muddler until they create a pulp. Add the mint leaves and crush them against the glass. Fill the glass with crushed ice. Add the rum and club soda, and stir gently. Garnish with a mint sprig and a lime wedge.

Kumquat Mojito

I tried a kumquat martini at The Hungry Cat, a restaurant in Los Angeles that offers an array of wonderful cocktails. After tasting the kumquat martini, I realized that kumquats go well with a variety of liquors . . . and beautifully with rum.

MAKES 1 DRINK

½ ounce freshly squeezed lime juice

2 teaspoons superfine sugar

5 kumquats, sliced and seeded

5 mint leaves, plus 1 sprig for garnish

Crushed ice

2 ounces white rum

1 ounce club soda

Put the lime juice and sugar in a highball or other glass. Stir until the sugar is dissolved. Add the kumquats and mint leaves and crush or muddle them against the glass with the back of a spoon or a muddler. Fill the glass with crushed ice. Add the rum and club soda, and stir gently. Garnish with a mint sprig.

Kiwi Mojito

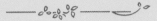

THEY'LL BE DRINKING THIS TANGY FAVORITE DOWN
UNDER IN NO TIME. IT'S A KEEPER!

MAKES 1 DRINK

½ cup peeled, cubed kiwi, plus one ¼-inch peeled slice for garnish (optional)

½ ounce freshly squeezed lime juice

1 ½ teaspoons superfine sugar

5 mint leaves, plus 1 sprig for garnish

Crushed ice

2 ounces white rum

1 ounce club soda

Place the cubed kiwi in a blender. Blend the fruit until it's smooth, about 2 minutes. (If desired, strain the liquid through a fine mesh sieve to remove the kiwi seeds.) Put the lime juice and sugar in a highball or other glass. Stir until the sugar is dissolved. Add the mint leaves and crush or muddle them against the glass with the back of a spoon or a muddler. Fill the glass with crushed ice. Add the pulverized kiwi, then the rum and club soda, and stir vigorously. Slice the kiwi round halfway through (if using). Place it on the side of the glass, and garnish with a mint sprig.

Hibiscus Mojito

BRIGHT, BOLD HIBISCUS FLOWERS SPEAK OF THE TROP-
ICS. WHEN STEAMED, THEY MAKE A DELICIOUS TEA,
WHICH HAS A DELICATE FLORAL AROMA. HIBISCUS COOLER
(A COMBINATION OF HIBISCUS TEA AND CRANBERRY
JUICE) WORKS BEAUTIFULLY IN A MOJITO TO SOFTEN THE
FLAVORS AND GIVE IT A SUBTLE FINISH. YOU CAN FIND
HIBISCUS COOLER AT MOST GROCERY STORES, OR MAKE
YOUR OWN USING ONE PART HIBISCUS TEA TO TWO PARTS
CRANBERRY JUICE.

MAKES 1 DRINK

½ ounce freshly squeezed lime juice

1 teaspoon superfine sugar

5 mint leaves, plus 1 sprig for garnish

Crushed ice

4 ounces sweetened hibiscus cooler

2 ounces white rum

1 ounce club soda

1 lime wedge for garnish

Put the lime juice and sugar in a high-ball or other glass. Stir until the sugar is dissolved. Add the mint leaves and crush or muddle them against the glass with the back of a spoon or a muddler. Fill the glass with crushed ice. Add the hibiscus cooler, rum, and club soda, and stir gently. Garnish with a mint sprig and a lime wedge.

CALMING COOLERS

(NONALCOHOLIC)

THESE REFRESHING DRINKS ARE WONDERFUL FOR CHILDREN AND ADULTS ALIKE. THE BLENDED ONES ARE MORE DIFFICULT TO MAKE FOR A CROWD, THOUGH YOU CERTAINLY CAN BLEND A PITCHER OR TWO FOR TEN TO TWELVE PEOPLE. THE MIXED BEVERAGES CAN BE KEPT ON HAND FOR BEACH PICNICS, LARGER BACK-YARD BARBECUES, OR EVEN SUMMER CAMPING TRIPS.

Blended Creamy Tropical

WHETHER YOU HAVE IT FOR BREAKFAST OR LUNCH OR AS
A SNACK, THIS CREAMY, RICH SMOOTHIE WILL MAKE YOU
DREAM OF WHITE-SAND BEACHES, TANGERINE SUNSETS,
AND LARGE BRILLIANT-COLORED TROPICAL FLOWERS.
MAKE SURE TO PEEL THE BANANA BEFORE FREEZING IT.

MAKES 1 DRINK

½ frozen banana

¼ cup peeled, chopped fresh pineapple

¼ cup peeled, chopped mango

4 ounces coconut milk

4 ounces freshly squeezed orange juice

1 sprig mint for garnish

Place the fruit in a blender. Blend for 1 minute. Add the coconut milk and orange juice and blend until completely smooth and creamy. Pour into a chilled Collins glass and garnish with a mint sprig.

Blended White Nectarine Freeze

ONLY IN SUMMER DO WE GET DELICIOUS, JUICY WHITE
NECTARINES, AND WHAT SPECTACULAR SMOOTHIES THEY
MAKE!

MAKES 1 DRINK

½ ripe white nectarine,
peeled and chopped

8 ounces whole milk

1 tablespoon honey

1 tablespoon almond extract

3 ice cubes

Combine all the ingredients in a blender. Blend until completely smooth and creamy. Pour into a chilled Collins glass.

Blended Horchata

This popular Mexican and Spanish drink is made with rice and flavored with cinnamon. In this recipe, I use a dash of nutmeg to give it a slightly nutty flavor.

MAKES 1 DRINK

8 ounces water

4 tablespoons white rice

2 ounces evaporated (not sweetened condensed) milk

3 teaspoons sugar

¼ teaspoon ground cinnamon, plus a dash for dusting

Pinch nutmeg

4 ice cubes

Combine the water, rice, milk, sugar, cinnamon, and nutmeg in a glass jar, close it tightly, and let it rest at room temperature overnight.

Pour the mixture into a blender, blending until smooth, then strain into a mixing glass. Add the ice cubes to the blender, then pour in the strained rice milk. Blend until the mixture is smooth. Pour into a chilled Collins glass and dust with a dash of cinnamon.

Blended Melon Ball

THIS DRINK IS SUCCULENT AND HONEY-SWEET AND OH SO JUICY. AS A REJUVENATING REFRESHER, IT WILL GIVE YOU ALL THE ENERGY YOU NEED FOR THOSE SLUGGISH, HOT SUMMER DAYS.

MAKES 1 DRINK

¼ cup peeled, coarsely chopped honeydew, plus 1 melon ball for garnish

¼ cup peeled, coarsely chopped seedless watermelon, plus 1 melon ball for garnish

2 tablespoons peeled, coarsely chopped cantaloupe, plus 1 melon ball for garnish

4 ounces watermelon juice

½ ounce freshly squeezed lime juice

2 ice cubes

1 sprig mint or mint leaves for garnish

Combine the melons, watermelon juice, lime juice, and ice cubes in a blender. Blend until completely smooth. Pour into a chilled Collins glass. Spear the melon balls. Garnish with the melon balls and mint.

Blended Peach Cream

REMEMBER THOSE DELICIOUS CREAMSICLES FROM YOUR CHILDHOOD? WELL IMAGINE ONE THAT'S A LITTLE MORE EXOTIC BECAUSE IT'S PEACH RATHER THAN ORANGE, AND YOU CAN DRINK IT RATHER THAN LICK IT. DON'T HESITATE TO GET THAT BLENDER GOING! IF YOU'D LIKE TO MAKE THIS DRINK A BIT SWEETER, ADD HONEY TO TASTE.

MAKES 1 DRINK

½ cup peeled, coarsely chopped peach

4 ounces whole milk

1 ounce peach or apricot nectar

1 tablespoon cream

2 ice cubes

Combine the ingredients in a blender. Blend until completely smooth. Pour into a chilled Collins glass.

Blended Tart Strawberry

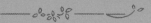

THIS COULD BE CALLED STRAWBERRY LEMONADE, BUT
IT'S NOT AS SWEET BECAUSE THE FRUIT ISN'T MUDDLED
WITH ANY SUGAR. IT'S ALSO BLENDED WITH ICE, WHICH
MAKES IT A PERFECT ICY DRINK FOR A HOT SUMMER DAY!

MAKES 1 DRINK

½ cup hulled, chopped fresh
strawberries, plus 2 whole
for garnish

4 ounces lemonade

2 ice cubes

Combine the ½ cup strawberries,
lemonade, and ice in a blender. Blend
until completely smooth. Pour into a
chilled Collins glass. Cut the whole strawberries halfway up from the bottom.
Garnish by placing the strawberries
on the side of the glass.

Blueberry Crush

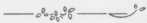

IF YOU LOVE BLUEBERRIES, THIS IS THE SUMMER DRINK
FOR YOU! IT'S FULL OF FRESH BLUEBERRY FLAVOR AND
LOTS OF ANTIOXIDANTS.

MAKES 1 DRINK

8 ounces unsweetened blue-berry or cranberry juice

½ cup blueberries

2 teaspoons Simple Syrup (page 16)

1 teaspoon freshly squeezed lime juice

Ice cubes

Sparkling water (optional)

Combine the blueberry juice, blueber-ries, simple syrup, and lime juice in a blender. Blend until the mixture is smooth. Pour over ice in a chilled Collins glass. Add sparkling water if desired to make the crush a little lighter.

Lime-Apricot Elixir

YOU'LL ENJOY THIS LIGHT, SPARKLING BEVERAGE ON A HOT SUMMER AFTERNOON SO MUCH THAT YOU MAY CONTINUE MAKING THEM INTO THE EVENING. IT IS BOTH THIRST QUENCHING AND DELICIOUS.

MAKES 1 DRINK

Ice cubes

8 ounces apricot nectar

½ ounce freshly squeezed lime juice

Sparkling water

1 sprig mint or 1 apricot slice for garnish

Fill a Collins glass with ice. Pour the nectar and lime juice over the ice. Add sparkling water until it reaches the top of the glass. Garnish with a mint sprig or apricot slice.

Green Tea Fizz

INSTEAD OF MAKING A STANDARD ICED TEA, WHY NOT
JAZZ IT UP A LITTLE? THIS VERSION USES GREEN TEA,
SPARKLING WATER, AND A LITTLE GRAPE JUICE FOR
SWEETENER—MAKING IT A SUBTLE, HEALTHY, AND
EFFERVESCENT VERSION OF A SUMMER CLASSIC.

MAKES 1 DRINK

8 ounces water

2 green tea bags

¼ cup chopped fresh mint leaves

5 ounces white grape juice

¼ lemon, thinly sliced

Ice cubes

Sparkling water

Place the water in a tea kettle or small saucepan and bring to a boil. In a heat-safe jar or pitcher, place the tea bags and the mint. Pour the boiling water over the tea and mint. Let steep for at least 5 minutes. Remove the tea bags, but leave the mint. Let the tea cool to room temperature. Add the grape juice and lemon slices. Place a handful of ice in a Collins glass. Fill the glass with the green tea mixture. Finish with a splash of sparkling water.

Limeade-Mint Icy

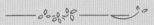

IF YOU LOVE THE TASTE OF A MOJITO, BUT DON'T WANT
THE ALCOHOL, THIS LIMEADE WILL GIVE YOU ALL THE
FLAVOR WITHOUT THE PUNCH.

MAKES 1 DRINK

4 large juicy limes, halved

3 tablespoons coarsely
chopped fresh mint

2 teaspoons superfine sugar

1 cup crushed ice

Sparkling water

Juice the limes into a mixing glass.
Add the mint and sugar and crush or
muddle the mixture against the glass
with the back of a spoon or a muddler.
Fill a Collins glass nearly full with ice
and the lime mixture. Finish with
sparkling water. Stir.

Pomegranate Tingle

THE GORGEOUS CRIMSON COLOR ALONE IS ENOUGH TO
MAKE YOU WANT A SIP OF THIS DRINK, BUT WAIT UNTIL
YOU TASTE THE CITRUS MIXED WITH THE TART, EARTHY
FLAVORS OF POMEGRANATE . . . IT'S SIMPLY DELICIOUS.

MAKES 1 DRINK

Ice cubes

8 ounces pomegranate juice

½ ounce purchased tangerine
or orange syrup

2 teaspoons freshly squeezed
lime juice

Sparkling water

1 lime slice for garnish

Place a handful of ice into a Collins
glass. Pour in the pomegranate juice,
tangerine syrup, and lime juice. Finish
with a splash of sparkling water.
Garnish with a lime slice.

South Sea Breeze

THIS LIGHT, ELEGANT DRINK IS TROPICAL WITHOUT BEING AS FILLING AS MANY TROPICAL CONCOCTIONS. IT'S A LOVELY BEVERAGE TO SERVE AT AN OUTDOOR LUNCHEON WITH SALADS AND COLD FISH.

MAKES 1 DRINK

Ice cubes

2 ounces coconut milk

2 ounces freshly squeezed lime juice

4 ounces guava nectar

Sparkling water

1 lime slice for garnish

Put a handful of ice in a cocktail shaker. Add the coconut milk, lime juice, and guava nectar. Shake the ingredients several times. Pour into a chilled highball glass and top with sparkling water. Garnish with a lime slice.

MODERN COCKTAILS

IF YOU'RE LOOKING FOR SOMETHING DIFFERENT TO ADD TO YOUR DRINK REPERTOIRE, LOOK NO FURTHER. THESE COCKTAILS TAKE INSPIRATION FROM THE CLASSICS AND PUSH THEM A LITTLE FURTHER WITH UNUSUAL COMBINATIONS OF INGREDIENTS LIKE FLAVORED VODKAS, HERBAL SYRUPS, AND SAKES. PICK A COUPLE TO SERVE AT A SUMMER COCKTAIL PARTY— YOUR GUESTS WILL LOVE THEIR LINGERING, EXOTIC FLAVORS.

Tangerine Dream

Here's a new take on a Cosmopolitan. Instead of cranberry I add a little tangerine juice, which gives it that playful, summery feel and color.

MAKES 1 DRINK

Ice cubes

1 ounce freshly squeezed tangerine juice

1 ounce vodka

½ ounce Cointreau

1 teaspoon freshly squeezed lime juice

1 tangerine slice for garnish

Optionally, salt the rim of a chilled martini glass (see page 39).

Put a handful of ice in a cocktail shaker. Pour the tangerine juice, vodka, Cointreau, and lime juice over the ice. Shake until very cold. Strain into the prepared glass or a chilled martini glass. Garnish with a tangerine slice.

Rose Martini

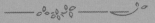

IF YOU'RE LOOKING FOR A ROMANTIC COCKTAIL TO WOO THE ONE YOU LOVE, LOOK NO FURTHER. THIS SUPER-DRY COCKTAIL IS SOPHISTICATED TO SIP AND BEAUTIFUL TO BEHOLD. IT'S LOVELY GARNISHED WITH PINK AND RED ROSE PETALS.

MAKES 1 DRINK

Ice cubes

1 ounce vodka

1 ounce dry rosé wine

1 ounce cranberry juice

½ ounce freshly squeezed lemon juice

Edible pink and red rose petals for garnish

Put a handful of ice in a cocktail shaker. Pour the vodka, wine, cranberry juice, and lemon juice over the ice. Shake until very cold. Strain into a chilled martini or other glass. Garnish with edible rose petals.

Kumquatini

THIS TART, ELEGANT COCKTAIL SMELLS LIKE ORANGE
BLOSSOMS AND TASTES LIKE A CITRUS DREAM.

MAKES 1 DRINK

1 ounce Simple Syrup
(page 16)

5 kumquats, sliced and seeded,
plus 2 whole for garnish

Ice cubes

1 ounce mandarin- or orange-
flavored vodka

1 tablespoon freshly
squeezed lemon juice

Put the simple syrup and sliced
kumquats in a mixing glass and crush
or muddle them with the back of a
spoon or muddler. Make sure that
the kumquats have been pressed
and pulverized on the side of the
glass. When the glass is filled with
large chunks of the fruit, set it aside.

Put a handful of ice in a cocktail shaker.
Pour the kumquat–simple syrup
mixture, vodka, and lemon juice over
the ice. Shake until very cold. Strain
into a chilled martini or wineglass.
Garnish with a spear of the remaining
2 kumquats.

Melontini

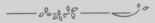

A MELON MARTINI? JUST TRY IT AND YOU'LL NEVER
QUESTION THIS SUBLIME COMBINATION AGAIN.

MAKES 1 DRINK

Ice cubes

1 ½ ounces vodka

¾ ounce Midori or other
melon-flavored liqueur

½ ounce pineapple juice

1 teaspoon freshly squeezed
lemon juice

1 lime slice for garnish

Put a handful of ice in a cocktail shaker.
Pour the vodka, Midori, pineapple juice,
and lemon juice over the ice. Shake until
very cold. Strain into a chilled martini
or wineglass. Cut the round of lime
halfway through. Rest it on the side of
the glass.

Cucumber-Lime Saketini

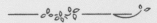

THE IDEA OF USING CUCUMBER IN A DRINK MAY SEEM ODD, BUT IT IMPARTS A CLEAN, FRESH FLAVOR WITHOUT THE ACIDITY OR BOLDNESS OF MOST FRUIT. WHEN IT'S COMBINED WITH CITRUS, CUCUMBER PLAYS DOWN THE TARTNESS, CREATING A DELICATE, ELEGANT COCKTAIL.

MAKES 1 DRINK

Five 2-inch slices cucumber, peeled, plus 1 slice for garnish (optional)

1½ ounces freshly squeezed lime juice

1½ teaspoons Simple Syrup (page 16)

Ice cubes

2 ounces dry sake

1 lime slice for garnish

In a mixing glass, combine the cucumber, lime juice, and simple syrup. Crush or muddle the cucumber against the glass with the back of a spoon or muddler.

Put a handful of ice in a cocktail shaker. Pour the sake and cumber-lime mixture over the ice. Shake until very cold. Strain into a chilled martini or wine-glass. Garnish with a lime slice and a cucumber slice (if using).

Lychee Gimlet

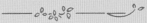

You could be in Fiji or Bora Bora or maybe just in your backyard longing for a vacation . . . if so, just sip one of these exotic beauties and you'll feel miles and miles away from home. If you can't find lychee nectar, buy lychees in syrup form. Put ½ can in the blender until smooth and then pour through a fine mesh sieve. The strained liquid is lychee nectar.

MAKES 1 DRINK

1 lime wedge

Superfine sugar

Ice cubes

2½ ounces lychee nectar

1½ ounces freshly squeezed lime juice

1 ounce gin

1 teaspoon Simple Syrup (page 16)

1 edible pansy or violet for garnish (optional)

Moisten the outer rim of a chilled martini or wineglass with the lime wedge. Spread several teaspoons of sugar on a shallow plate and dip the glass in the sugar, covering it with a light band.

Put a handful of ice in a cocktail shaker. Pour the lychee nectar, lime juice, gin, and simple syrup over the ice. Shake until very cold. Strain into the prepared glass. Garnish with an edible flower (if using).

Lemongrass Lemonade

—⚬⚭⚬—⚬

Instead of a sweet Lemon Drop, go for its Asian cousin . . . a lemongrass lemonade. Though it tastes light, tart, and smooth, don't be fooled—it's no plain lemonade.

MAKES 1 DRINK

Ice cubes

2 ounces vodka

2 ounces Lemongrass Syrup (page 16)

2 ounces freshly squeezed lemon juice

1 lemon slice for garnish

1 sprig mint for garnish

Put a handful of ice in a cocktail shaker. Pour the vodka, lemongrass syrup, and lemon juice over the ice. Shake until very cold. Strain into a chilled martini or wineglass. Garnish with a lemon slice and mint sprig.

Asian Pear Martini

ELEGANT, RESTRAINED, AND CHIC—IS IT POSSIBLE THAT A COCKTAIL CAN BE JUST LIKE A PERSON? ABSOLUTELY. AND JUST LIKE A PERSON, A COCKTAIL CAN KEEP YOU GUESSING. THE GINGER IMPARTS A SWEET, SPICY, UNIQUE FLAVOR THAT WILL TASTE LIKE NOTHING YOU'VE EVER HAD BEFORE.

MAKES 1 DRINK

Ice cubes

2 ounces dry sake

2 ounces pear juice

1 slice Asian pear for garnish (optional)

1 piece candied (crystallized) ginger

Put a handful of ice in a cocktail shaker. Pour the sake and pear juice over the ice. Shake until very cold. Strain into a chilled martini or wineglass. Make a slit in the Asian pear (if using) and rest it on the side of the glass. Drop the candied ginger into the drink.

Ginger Saketini

THIS EXOTIC COCKTAIL HAS A WONDERFUL COMPLEXITY, WITH ITS SUBTLE HEAT FROM THE GINGER AND ITS LIVELY, FRESH CITRUS UNDERTONES FROM THE GRAPEFRUIT AND LEMON.

MAKES 1 DRINK

Ice cubes

2 ounces dry sake

1½ ounces Ginger Syrup (page 16)

1 tablespoon freshly squeezed lemon juice

1 tablespoon freshly squeezed grapefruit juice

1 lemon slice for garnish

Put a handful of ice in a cocktail shaker. Pour the sake, ginger syrup, lemon juice, and grapefruit juice over the ice. Shake until very cold. Strain into a chilled martini or wineglass. Cut the round of lemon halfway through and rest it on the side of the glass.

Blackberry Vodka Gimlet

In August when the blackberries are big and sweet, this cocktail is unbeatable.

MAKES 1 DRINK

5 large blackberries

1½ ounces freshly squeezed lime juice

1 teaspoon Simple Syrup (page 16)

Ice cubes

1 ounce vodka

1 sprig mint for garnish

Combine the blackberries, lime juice, and simple syrup in a mixing glass. Crush or muddle the berries with the back of a spoon or muddler until they are mashed into the mixture.

Put a handful of ice in a cocktail shaker. Pour the vodka and blackberry mixture over the ice. Shake until very cold. Strain into a chilled martini or wine-glass. Garnish with a mint sprig.

Lemon-Rosemary Saketini

I USE THE SYRUP FOR THIS DRINK TO MAKE A REFRESHING SORBET, SO I THOUGHT WHY NOT TRY IT AS THE BASE FOR A COCKTAIL? THE ROSEMARY IMPARTS SUCH A BUTTERY SMOOTH, DELICATE FLAVOR THAT IS ONLY IMPROVED FURTHER BY THE SUBTLE, CRISP FLAVOR OF THE SAKE.

MAKES 1 DRINK

Ice cubes

2 ounces Lemon-Rosemary Syrup (page 16)

2 ounces dry sake

1 sprig rosemary for garnish

Put a handful of ice in a cocktail shaker. Pour the lemon-rosemary syrup and sake over the ice. Shake until very cold. Strain into a chilled martini or wineglass. Garnish with a rosemary sprig.

Blueberry-Limoncello Martini

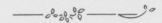

LIMONCELLO IS A LEMONY LIQUEUR THAT IS VERY POPU-LAR AMONG THE ITALIANS, PARTICULARLY ON CAPRI AND AT CAFÉS ALL OVER NAPLES. THE BLUEBERRIES ADD A PLAYFUL BURST OF FLAVOR TO THIS CITRUS-BASED COCKTAIL.

MAKES 1 DRINK

2 teaspoons freshly squeezed lemon juice

⅛ teaspoon superfine sugar

Ice cubes

1 ounce citron vodka

1 ounce limoncello

5 or 6 frozen blueberries

Combine the lemon juice and sugar in a mixing glass. Stir the mixture until the sugar dissolves. Put a handful of ice in a cocktail shaker. Pour the lemon mixture, vodka, and limoncello over the ice. Shake until very cold. Strain into a chilled martini or wineglass. Drop the blueberries in the drink.

INDEX

TABLE OF EQUIVALENTS

The exact equivalents in the following tables have been rounded for convenience.

Liquid/Dry Measures

U.S.	Metric
¼ teaspoon	1.25 milliliters
½ teaspoon	2.5 milliliters
1 teaspoon	5 milliliters
1 tablespoon (3 teaspoons)	15 milliliters
1 fluid ounce (2 tablespoons)	30 milliliters
¼ cup	60 milliliters
⅓ cup	80 milliliters
½ cup	120 milliliters
1 cup	240 milliliters
1 pint (2 cups)	480 milliliters
1 quart (4 cups, 32 ounces)	960 milliliters
1 gallon (4 quarts)	3.84 liters
1 ounce (by weight)	28 grams
1 pound	454 grams
2.2 pounds	1 kilogram

Length

U.S.	Metric
⅛ inch	3 millimeters
¼ inch	6 millimeters
½ inch	12 millimeters
1 inch	2.5 centimeters

Liquid Measurements

Bar spoon = ½ ounce	1 cup = 8 ounces
1 teaspoon = ⅙ ounce	1 pint = 16 ounces
1 tablespoon = ½ ounce	1 quart = 32 ounces
2 tablespoons (pony) = 1 ounce	750 ml bottle = 25.4 ounces
3 tablespoons (jigger)= 1½ ounces	1 liter bottle = 33.8 ounces
¼ cup = 2 ounces	
⅜ cup = 3 ounces	1 medium lemon = 3 tablespoons juice
½ cup = 4 ounces	1 medium lime = 2 tablespoons juice
⅝ cup = 5 ounces	1 medium orange = ⅓ cup juice
¾ cup = 6 ounces